FAVOURITE
BISCUIT
RECIPES

Traditional
Plain and Fancy
Tea-Time Treats

SALMON

Index

Cover pictures: *front:* Sutton Valence Windmill, Kent by J. C. T. Willis RI
back: Lower Slaughter Watermill, Glos. by H. Sylvester Stannard RA
title page: Elmley Castle Watermill, Worcs. by A. R. Quinton

Devon Clotted Cream Biscuits

This delicious, light-textured biscuit recipe makes use of wonderful thick,
yellow Devonshire Cream for its fat content, instead of the usual butter.

8 oz. thick farmhouse clotted cream

1 lb. flour   **1 large egg**   **4 oz. caster sugar**

1-2 tablespoons milk

Set oven to 400°F or Mark 6. Flour a baking sheet. Place the clotted cream in a large mixing bowl and sieve in the flour. Add the egg, stirring with a round-ended knife until the mixture resembles fine breadcrumbs. Add 3 oz. of the sugar and enough milk to make a pastry consistency. Roll out thinly on a lightly floured surface and cut into rounds. Sprinkle with the remaining caster sugar. Place on the baking sheet and bake for approximately 15 minutes until pale golden in colour. Cool slightly before transferring to a wire rack.

Dorset Fair Gingerbreads

Although called 'gingerbread' these are, in fact, crisp ginger biscuits which were sold at Dorset country fairs.

3 oz. butter	6 oz. flour
3 oz. soft brown sugar	1 level teaspoon baking powder
4 tablespoons golden syrup, warmed	1 level teaspoon bicarbonate of soda

1 rounded teaspoon ground ginger

Set oven to 400°F or Mark 6. Grease baking trays. Cream together the butter and sugar in a warmed bowl and add the golden syrup, flour and all other dry ingredients. Mix well to form a firm dough. Roll out on a lightly floured surface, form into about 25-30 small balls and place 3 inches apart on the baking trays. Cook for approximately 10 minutes until golden brown. Cool slightly before transferring to a wire rack.

Wafers

Light and crispy wafers date back to Shakespeare's time and, like the later brandy snaps, were a popular sweetmeat to be enjoyed on market days and at fairs. Traditionally, they should be eaten hot.

4 oz flour   2 oz butter, softened
Pinch salt   ¹/₂ fl. oz double cream
1 level tablespoon clear honey

Set oven to 300°F or Mark 2. Lightly butter a baking sheet. Sieve the flour and salt together into a bowl and rub in the butter until the mixture resembles fine breadcrumbs. Stir in the cream and honey. Roll out thinly on a lightly floured surface and cut into small rounds. Place the wafers on the baking sheet, allowing plenty of room between each one and bake for 15 to 20 minutes until crisp. Transfer to a wire rack to cool.

Oat Biscuits

Crisp, oatmeal biscuits with a delightful crunchy, open texture.

4 oz. butter	**6 oz. flour**
4 oz. brown sugar	**1 teaspoon bicarbonate of soda**
6 oz. rolled oats	**2 tablespoons milk**

Set oven to 300°F or Mark 2. Grease baking sheets. Cream the butter and the sugar together in a bowl. Mix in the oats and sift the flour and the bicarbonate of soda together into the mixture and mix thoroughly. Add sufficient milk to form the mixture into a stiffish dough. Turn out on to a floured surface, roll out the dough thinly and cut into rounds with a 2 inch cutter. Put on to the greased baking sheets and bake for approximately 20 minutes or until golden brown. Transfer to a wire rack to cool. Makes 36 biscuits.

Honey Fruit Biscuits

These delicious, fruity biscuits combine clear honey, chopped nuts and chocolate chips.

1 level teaspoon clear honey	1 oz. chocolate chips
4 oz. butter	Grated rind of 1 orange
4 oz. soft brown sugar	2 oz. finely chopped nuts
1 large egg	Pinch of salt

8 oz. self raising flour

Set oven to 350°F or Mark 4. Grease baking sheets. Cream the butter and sugar together in a mixing bowl until soft. Beat in the egg and honey and stir in the nuts, grated rind, chocolate chips and salt. Sieve in the flour and mix well. Divide the mixture into balls each the size of a walnut. Place about 2 inches apart on the baking sheets and flatten slightly with a floured fork. Bake for 10-15 minutes until pale brown. Leave to cool for a few minutes and then transfer to a wire rack. Makes about 36 biscuits.

Windmills by the River Thurne, Norfolk by A. Heaton Cooper

Suffolk Rusks

These plain, twice baked rusks, are served with cheese as an alternative to biscuits.
They also go well with Bloater Paste or with butter and jam at teatime.

8 oz. self raising flour   **3 oz. butter**
Pinch of salt   **1 egg, beaten**
A little milk or water

Set oven to 450°F or Mark 8. Grease a baking sheet. Sift the flour and salt together into a bowl, then rub in the butter until the mixture resembles fine breadcrumbs. Stir in the beaten egg and sufficient milk or water to make a smooth dough. Roll out on a lightly floured surface to about 1 inch in thickness then cut into 2½ inch rounds. Place on the baking sheet and cook for 10 minutes. Remove from the oven and split in half. Reduce the oven temperature to 375°F or Mark 5. Return the rusks to the baking sheet, cut side upwards, and cook for a further 10 to 15 minutes until crisp and golden brown. Cool on a wire rack.

Butterscotch Biscuits

Rather more a cookie than a biscuit, with a rich, butterscotch flavour.

8 oz. light brown sugar	**1 egg, beaten**
4 oz. butter	**12 oz. self raising flour**
1 teaspoon vanilla essence	**½ teaspoon salt**

Set oven to 350°F or Mark 4. Grease or line a baking sheet. Melt the sugar, butter and vanilla essence together in a saucepan very gently over a low heat. Remove from the heat. When the mixture has cooled add the beaten egg and mix together. Sift the flour and salt into a bowl. Make a well in the centre and pour in the cooled egg/fat/sugar mixture. Knead into a stiff dough. This will be fairly dry, but it needs no extra moisture. Roll out to ½ inch thickness on a floured surface and cut out the biscuits with a 2 inch cutter. Place on the baking sheet with sufficient space to allow them to spread. Bake for 20 minutes until light golden in colour. Allow to cool slightly before transferring to a wire rack. Makes 20-24 biscuits.

Picnic Slices

In this recipe a coconut and fruity mixture is layered on to a melted chocolate base.

8 oz. plain or milk cooking chocolate	1 egg, beaten
2 oz. butter	4 oz. dessicated coconut
4 oz. caster sugar	2 oz. sultanas

2 oz. glacé cherries, chopped

Set oven to 300°F or Mark 2. Grease a Swiss Roll tin. Break the chocolate into pieces and place in bowl over hot water. When the chocolate is melted, pour into the bottom of the Swiss Roll tin and leave to set. Meanwhile, cream the butter and sugar together in a bowl and add the beaten egg, coconut, sultanas and chopped cherries. Mix well and spread evenly over the chocolate base. Bake for 30 minutes until golden brown. Leave to cool slightly in the tin then cut into slices with a sharp knife and transfer to a wire rack.

Shrewsbury Biscuits

A traditional English biscuit. Sometimes known as Shrewsbury Cakes or Shrewsbury Easter Biscuits, they have been made since the 16th century and traditionally were offered to notable visitors to Shrewsbury. There are other traditional flavour variations, including mixed spice, caraway seeds, rose water and currants.

4 oz. butter	**2 egg yolks**
5 oz. caster sugar	**8 oz. flour**

Finely grated rind of a lemon

Set oven to 350°F or Mark 4. Lightly grease a baking sheet. Cream the butter and sugar together in a bowl until light and fluffy, then beat in the egg yolks. Add the flour and the lemon rind and mix, forming a fairly firm dough. Turn out on to a lightly floured surface, knead lightly for one minute, then roll out to about ¼ inch thick. Using a fluted 2½ inch cutter, cut into rounds and place on the baking sheet. Bake for 12-15 minutes until golden and firm to the touch. Cool on a wire rack. Makes about 20 biscuits.

Lancashire Nuts

Flattened drop biscuits sandwiched with a smooth, butter cream filling.

4 oz. butter, softened	4 oz. flour
4 oz. caster sugar	½ teaspoon baking powder
1 egg, beaten	4 oz. cornflour

BUTTER CREAM

3 oz. butter, softened	6 oz. icing sugar

A little warm milk

Set oven to 325°F or Mark 3. Well grease a baking sheet. In a bowl, cream the butter and sugar together until fluffy, then beat in the egg, a little at a time. Sift together the flour, baking powder and cornflour and fold into the mixture to form a smooth, stiff dough. On a lightly floured surface, using the hands, roll the mixture into balls each about the size of a walnut and place on the baking sheet. Bake for 25 to 30 minutes until golden. Cool on a wire rack. For the butter cream, beat the butter until fluffy, then add the icing sugar, beating until smooth and adding a little warm milk, if necessary, to produce a spreading consistency. Use to sandwich the biscuits in pairs. Makes about 16 to 20 biscuits.

Almond Shortbread Biscuits

A deliciously crisp shortbread that keeps well.

5 oz. butter   2 oz. cornflour
6 oz. flour   1 oz. ground almonds
3 oz. caster sugar

Set oven to 350°F or Mark 4. Grease a baking sheet. Cream the butter in a mixing bowl. Sift together the flour and cornflour and add, with the almonds and sugar, to the butter. Work the ingredients together with the hands. Turn out on to a very lightly floured surface and finish kneading until the dough is smooth. Divide the dough in half and shape and press into two rounds each ¼ inch thick on the greased baking sheet. Prick well with a fork and mark each circle into six triangles. Bake for about 25-30 minutes until lightly coloured. Allow to cool slightly before cutting and then place on a wire rack to finish cooling.

Brill Windmill, Buckinghamshire by Sutton Palmer RI

Cheddar Cheese Straps

Cheese straws are an ever popular savoury snack. They look very attractive if one end is dipped in paprika and the other in very finely chopped parsley when cold.

4 oz. flour	**2 oz. butter**
Pinch of salt	**2 oz. strong Cheddar cheese, finely grated**
½ teaspoon mustard powder	**1 egg, beaten**

Paprika and finely chopped parsley (optional)

Set oven to 400°F or Mark 6. Lightly flour a baking sheet. Place the flour, salt and mustard powder into a bowl. Rub in the butter until the mixture resembles breadcrumbs. Stir in the cheese and add enough beaten egg to form a firm dough. Turn out on to a lightly floured surface and knead lightly until smooth. Roll out to a rectangle ¼ inch thick and cut into strips 3 inches long by ½ inch wide. Place on the baking sheet and cook for 10-15 minutes until pale golden in colour. Cool on a wire rack. If preferred, they can be twisted into spirals before baking.

Rout Biscuits

These sweetmeats were popular accompaniments to a glass of wine or sherry at routs or fashionable gatherings in the 18th and 19th centuries. A Middlesex recipe.

6 oz. caster sugar   **A few drops of almond or**
6 oz. ground almonds   **ratafia essence**
2 egg whites   **A little beaten egg yolk, to glaze**
Small pieces of glacé cherry, angelica or flaked almond for decoration

Set oven to 350°F or Mark 4. Grease a baking sheet. Combine the sugar and ground almonds and essence together in a bowl until evenly coloured. Gradually stir in the egg whites, stirring until the mixture is smooth and firm. Spoon into a piping bag fitted with a small rosette, star or scroll nozzle. Set the biscuits well apart on the baking sheet and pipe each one according to inclination. Decorate with a piece of cherry, angelica or flaked almond, brush lightly with beaten egg yolk to give a golden glaze and bake for 6-7 minutes. Cool on a wire rack.

Essex Shortcakes

These shortcake biscuits contain currants and are sprinkled with sugar before baking.

9 oz. self raising flour	**1 oz. lard**
2 oz. sugar	**1½ oz. currants**
3 oz. butter or margarine	**1 fl. oz. milk**

Sugar for sprinkling

Set oven to 400°F or Mark 6. Grease a baking sheet. Sift the flour into a bowl and add the sugar. Rub in the butter or margarine and the lard, then add the currants. Gradually mix in the milk until the mixture binds together. Gently roll out the mixture to ½ inch thickness on a lightly floured surface and then cut into slices. Place on the baking sheet and sprinkle sugar over the top of the biscuits. Bake for about 10 minutes until pale golden brown. Remove the biscuits from the baking sheet while still warm and transfer to a wire rack to cool. Makes about 12-16 slices.

Wareham Bears

Beloved by children, these Dorset biscuits can be made either with a plain shortbread or a chocolate shortbread mixture, as desired.

5 oz. flour	**4 oz. butter, cut into small pieces**
1 oz. cornflour	**2 oz. caster sugar**
OR	**2 tablespoons milk**
5½ oz. flour	**Currants and glacé cherries**
½ oz. cocoa powder	**for decoration**

Set oven to 325°F or Mark 3. Lightly flour a baking sheet. Sieve the flour and cornflour or flour and cocoa powder into a large bowl. Add the butter and rub into the flour until the mixture resembles fine breadcrumbs. Stir in the sugar, add the milk and bind the mixture together by hand to form a ball of dough. Roll out the dough to ¼ inch thickness on a lightly floured surface. Cut out with a bear shaped cutter and transfer to the baking sheet. Decorate with currants and pieces of glacé cherry to make eyes, nose etc. Bake for 30 minutes until pale golden brown. Cool on the baking tray for 5 minutes before transferring to a wire rack.

Chocolate Coconut Fingers

This simple recipe makes delicious, iced biscuits which are ideal for coffee mornings and fêtes.

4 oz. butter or margarine	**4 oz. self raising flour**
2 oz. granulated sugar	**2 oz. desiccated coconut**

2 teaspoons cocoa powder

ICING

4 oz. icing sugar	**1 teaspoon cocoa powder**	**Water to mix**

Set oven to 350°F or Mark 4. Grease a 7 inch square shallow tin. Melt the butter or margarine and sugar together in a pan. Stir in the flour, coconut and cocoa powder. Turn out the mixture into the tin, spread and press down evenly and bake for 15-20 minutes. Ice immediately with glacé icing made by mixing together the icing sugar, cocoa powder and a very little water. Cut into fingers when the icing has set and before the base hardens too much and transfer to a wire rack.

Easter Biscuits

*These soft, fruit filled biscuits with a sugary topping were traditionally
eaten at Easter with Simnel Cake.*

3 oz. butter, softened	**½ oz. mixed peel**
3 oz. caster sugar	**Pinch of mixed spice**
1 egg yolk	**6 oz. flour**
2 oz. currants	**A little milk**

Egg white and caster sugar to glaze

Set oven to 350°F or Mark 4. Grease a baking sheet. Cream the butter and sugar
together in a bowl until light and fluffy. Add the egg yolk, currants, peel, spice and
flour and mix with sufficient milk to form a stiff dough. Turn out on to a lightly
floured surface and roll out thinly. Cut into 2½-3 inch rounds with a cutter and place
on the baking sheet. Bake for 10 minutes, remove from the oven, brush with the egg
white, sprinkle with caster sugar and return to the oven. Bake for a further 5-10
minutes until light, golden brown. Transfer to a wire rack to cool.

Blackburn Cracknells

Perfectly plain, smooth textured biscuits from Lancashire, which are ideal for eating with any tangy and well flavoured cheese.

½ lb. flour	**½ oz. baking powder**
2 oz. lard	**¼ pint warm milk**

Set oven to 325°F or Mark 3. Grease a baking sheet. Sift the flour into a bowl and rub in the lard until the mixture resembles fine breadcrumbs, then add the baking powder and milk. Mix to form a smooth dough, then turn out on a lightly floured surface and knead well. Roll out to ⅛ inch thick and cut into 2½-3 inch rounds. Place on the baking sheet and prick with a fork. Cook for 30 minutes or until golden in colour. Cool on a wire rack and store in an airtight tin. Serve plain or buttered. Makes about 20-30 biscuits.

Wakes Cakes

Wakes Week was an autumn festival in the North of England to cheer people before the coming of the long dark nights, featuring merry-go-rounds, hawkers, stalls with ribbons and gingerbread and, of course, Wakes Cakes.

8 oz. butter	**½ teaspoon baking powder**
6 oz. caster sugar	**3 oz. currants**
1 egg, beaten	**½ oz. caraway seeds**
12 oz. flour	**Grated rind of 1 lemon**

Caster sugar to sprinkle

Set oven to 375°F or Mark 5. Grease a baking sheet. Cream the butter and sugar together in a bowl, add the beaten egg and mix in all the other ingredients to make a firm dough. Roll out thinly on a floured surface, cut into rounds with a 2½ inch cutter, sprinkle with sugar and place on the baking sheet. Bake for 10-15 minutes until lightly browned. They should be crisp and sweet like biscuits.

Gingerbread Men

An old-time favourite with children of all ages!

4 oz. butter	1 teaspoon orange juice
4 oz. soft brown sugar	8 oz. self-raising flour
1 tablespoon black treacle	2 teaspoons ground ginger
1 tablespoon golden syrup	1 level teaspoon mixed spice

Glacé icing for decoration

Set oven to 350°F or Mark 4. Grease and flour baking sheets. Cream together in a bowl the butter, sugar, treacle, syrup and orange juice. Add the dry ingredients. Knead well with the fingers. Roll out thinly on a lightly floured surface. Cut out gingerbread men using a shaped cutter (available from cookware shops) or cut round a cardboard template. Place on the baking sheets and bake for 10-15 minutes. Allow to cool for a few minutes before removing from the sheets. Decorate with white or coloured glacé icing.

Ladies Fingers

Also known as Savoy Biscuits or Sponge Fingers, these piped biscuits are particularly useful for making desserts and iced puddings.

2 eggs	**10 oz. flour**
6 oz. caster sugar	**½ teaspoon lemon essence**

Set oven to 425°F or Mark 7. Grease a baking sheet. Break the eggs into a basin over a pan of hot water, add the sugar and essence and beat well for ¼ hour until the mixture thickens and turns pale. Gradually sift in the flour, folding and cutting lightly into the mixture. Put the mixture into an icing bag and pipe the biscuits, about 3 inches long, on to the baking sheet. Bake for slightly less than 10 minutes. Be sure to watch the time very carefully, as a few seconds over the proper time will scorch and spoil the biscuits. Cool on a wire rack.

Stanhope Firelighters

A form of flapjack which is traditional to County Durham.

8 oz. rolled oats   **4 oz. brown sugar**
8 oz. butter or margarine, melted   **4 oz. white sugar**

Set oven to 350°F or Mark 4. Well grease a Swiss Roll tin or shallow baking tin. Blend the oats and butter or margarine well together in a bowl. Mix the sugars together and stir into the mixture, combining well. Press the mixture evenly into the tin and bake for 25-30 minutes. Mark into squares in the tin while still hot and remove when cool.

Oaty Crumbles

Originally, black treacle would have been used in this recipe but, today, golden syrup is the more usual ingredient.

2 oz. caster sugar	4 oz. self raising flour
1 generous tablespoon golden syrup	½ teaspoon salt
4 oz. butter or margarine	4 oz. rolled oats

Oatmeal for sprinkling

Set oven to 350°F or Mark 4. Grease a 7 inch cake tin. Melt the sugar, syrup and butter or margarine in a saucepan and remove from the heat. Sift the flour and salt into a bowl and add the oats. Pour the cooled syrup mixture on to the dry ingredients. Mix well. Press the mixture evenly into the cake tin and sprinkle over with some oatmeal. Bake for 20 to 25 minutes until light golden brown. Mark into slices, allow to cool in the tin and then turn out and break up on a wire rack.

Thaxted Windmill, Essex by H. S. Merritt

Bosworth Jumbles

It is said the original recipe was dropped by Richard III's cook at the Battle of Bosworth Field. The name 'jumble' is derived from 'gemmel' which was an interlaced finger ring, which these biscuits are believed to resemble.

5 oz. butter	**10 oz. flour**
5 oz. sugar	**2 oz. ground almonds**
1 egg, beaten	**1 teaspoon grated lemon rind**

Set oven to 350°F or Mark 4. Grease 2 baking sheets. Cream the butter and sugar together in a bowl until light and fluffy, then add the egg. Fold in the flour, ground almonds and finely grated lemon rind to form a soft but firm dough. On a lightly floured surface, roll out the dough with the hands to form a long sausage about the thickness of a middle finger. Cut into pieces approximately 5 inches long and place, well apart, on the baking sheets, carefully curling the pieces into 'S' shapes. Bake for 12-15 minutes, then cool on a wire rack.

Digestive Biscuits

These wholemeal biscuits can be served plain or buttered together with cheese; they go well with the distinctive Blue Vinney Cheese from their native county of Dorset.

6 oz. self raising wholemeal flour	**3 oz. butter**
2 oz. fine oatmeal	**1 oz. soft brown sugar**
1 level teaspoon salt	**4 tablespoons milk**

Set oven to 375°F or Mark 5. Flour a baking sheet. Put the flour, oatmeal and salt into a bowl and rub in the butter until the mixture resembles breadcrumbs. Stir in the sugar and enough milk to bind to a firm dough. Roll out on a floured surface to ¼ inch thickness. Cut into 3 inch rounds and prick evenly all over with a fork. Transfer to the baking sheet and cook for approximately 20 minutes until lightly browned. Cool slightly before transferring to a wire rack.

Butter Drops

Butter Drops are delicious with that mid-morning cup of coffee.

4 oz. butter	**2 large eggs, beaten**
4 oz. caster sugar	**5 oz. flour**

½ level teaspoon baking powder

Set oven to 325°F or Mark 3. Grease baking sheets. Melt the butter slowly in a saucepan until it turns pale brown. Remove from the heat and leave to cool for 10 minutes, then beat in the sugar and the beaten eggs. Sift the flour and baking powder together and stir them in to the pan. Put teaspoonfuls of the mixture on each baking sheet, spaced well apart as they spread during cooking. Bake for about 20 minutes until they are golden brown round the edges. Transfer to a wire rack immediately.

Abernethy Biscuits

A plain, sweet biscuit flavoured with caraway seeds.

8 oz. flour	**3 oz. caster sugar**
½ teaspoon baking powder	**½ teaspoon caraway seeds**
3 oz. butter	**1 egg, beaten**

1 tablespoon milk

Set oven to 350°F or Mark 4. Grease a baking sheet. Sift the flour and baking powder into a bowl. Rub in the butter well until the mixture resembles breadcrumbs. Add the sugar and the caraway seeds. Add the beaten egg and the milk and mix thoroughly until it forms a sticky dough. Turn the dough on to a well floured surface and roll out thinly. Cut into rounds with a 2 inch biscuit cutter. Place on the baking sheet and cook for about 10-15 minutes until pale golden in colour.

Cressing Biscuits

These plain biscuits filled with a butter cream mixture, come from the Knights Templar village of Cressing near Braintree in Essex.

2 oz. butter or margarine	½ teaspoon bicarbonate of soda
2 oz. lard	1 teaspoon baking powder
3 oz. sugar	1 cup rolled oats
4 oz. flour	1 teaspoon hot water

1 teaspoon golden syrup

BUTTER CREAM

5 oz. icing sugar	3 oz. margarine	Vanilla essence

Set oven to 350°F or Mark 4. Grease a baking sheet. In a bowl, cream together the butter or margarine, lard and sugar. Sift the flour together with the bicarbonate of soda and the baking powder and mix into the creamed mixture, together with the oats, syrup and hot water. Form into 24 walnut size balls and cook, well spaced, on the baking sheet for 10-15 minutes. Transfer to a wire rack to cool. Make up the butter cream by beating together the icing sugar, margarine and a little vanilla essence and use to sandwich the biscuits in pairs when cold.

Uplands Biscuits

Sandwich biscuits filled with raspberry jam and topped with icing and a glacé cherry.

8 oz. butter or margarine	**10 oz. self raising flour**
5 oz. sugar	**2 oz. custard powder**
1 large egg, beaten	**Pinch of salt**

Home made raspberry jam
Glacé icing and glacé cherries

Set oven to 350°F or Mark 4. Grease baking sheets. Beat the butter or margarine and sugar together in a bowl until very soft. Stir in the beaten egg and the rest of the ingredients. Knead well with the fingers. Roll out on a lightly floured surface and cut out with a 2 inch plain biscuit cutter. Place on the baking sheets and bake for 10 minutes until pale brown. Transfer to a wire rack and when cold sandwich the biscuits in pairs with home made raspberry jam. Put a little white glacé icing on top of each biscuit and decorate with half a glacé cherry.

Cley-next-the-Sea Windmill, Norfolk by Martin Hardie RI

Coconut Cookies

These rough textured and dainty little biscuits are crisp with a slightly chewy centre.

2 egg whites   **4 oz. caster sugar**
6 oz. desiccated coconut

Set oven to 325°F or Mark 3. Line a baking sheet with baking parchment. Whisk the egg whites in a bowl until very stiff. Fold in the sugar and then add and fold in the coconut. Drop small dessertspoonsful of the mixture on to the baking sheet, leaving some room between each for expansion. Bake for about 15 minutes until lightly browned. Allow to cool slightly on the baking sheet and then transfer to a wire rack to get cold. Makes about 18-20 cookies.

Buttermere Biscuits

Cinnamon flavoured shortcake biscuits laced with currants, from the Lake District.

8 oz. flour	**1½ oz. currants**
Pinch of salt	**Grated rind of 1 lemon**
4 oz. butter	**½ level teaspoon baking powder**
4 oz. caster sugar	**Pinch of ground cinnamon**

1 large egg, beaten

Set oven to 350°F or Mark 4. Grease baking sheets. Sieve the flour and salt into a mixing bowl. Rub the butter into the flour until it resembles fine breadcrumbs. Add the sugar, currants, lemon rind, baking powder and cinnamon. Bind with the beaten egg and knead the mixture lightly. Roll out to ¼ inch thickness on a lightly floured surface and cut with a 2 inch fluted biscuit cutter. Place on the baking sheets and bake for 15-20 minutes until pale brown. Cool on a wire rack. Makes about 30 biscuits.

Garibaldi Biscuits

Currants sandwiched in pastry give these biscuits their popular name of 'squashed-fly' biscuits.

7 oz. flour	2 oz. butter
1 oz. cornflour	1 egg yolk
2 oz. caster sugar	A little milk
Pinch of salt	4 oz. currants

Egg white to glaze

Set oven to 400°F or Mark 6. Grease a baking sheet. Sift the flour and cornflour into a bowl with the sugar and salt. Rub in the butter until the mixture resembles breadcrumbs. Add the egg yolk and mix to a stiffish dough with sufficient milk. Turn out on to a floured surface and roll out thinly to a long, thin rectangle. Trim the edges square and sprinkle one half of the dough evenly with the currants. Fold over the dough and press the edges together. Roll with a floured rolling pin to about ⅛ inch thick, cut into convenient squares or rectangles and brush with egg white to glaze. Place on the baking sheet and bake for 15 minutes until golden brown. Cool on a wire rack.

Cornish Ginger Fairings

These spicy ginger biscuits were traditionally sold at Cornish country fairs and are today popular with visitors to the county.

4 oz. flour	1 teaspoon mixed spice
1 teaspoon baking powder	1 oz. grated lemon peel
1 teaspoon bicarbonate of soda	2 oz. brown sugar
1 teaspoon ground cinnamon	2 oz. butter or margarine
1 teaspoon ground ginger	2 tablespoons golden syrup, warmed

Set oven to 350°F or Mark 4. Grease a baking sheet. Mix the baking powder, bicarbonate of soda, the spices and lemon peel together in a bowl, sieve in the flour and add the sugar. Mix thoroughly. Rub in the butter or margarine. Add the warmed syrup, using the fingers to combine to a smooth paste, then roll the final mix into small balls, each about the size of a walnut. Place the balls on the baking sheet, leaving plenty of room between each one. Cook for about 15 minutes then reduce temperature to 325°F or Mark 3 and finish cooking for 5-10 minutes so that the biscuits sink and crack into their familiar form. Transfer to a wire rack to cool.

Ayrshire Shortbread

This Scottish shortbread recipe differs from some others by the addition of egg yolk and double cream to the usual ingredients.

4 oz. ground rice   **4 oz. caster sugar**
4 oz. flour   **1 egg yolk, beaten**
4 oz. butter   **1 tablespoon double cream**
1 drop vanilla essence

Set oven to 350°F or Mark 4. Grease a baking sheet. Sift the flour and ground rice into a bowl. Rub in the butter and add the caster sugar. Stir in the beaten egg yolk, the cream and the vanilla essence to bind the mixture. Knead well on a floured surface to a stiff consistency. Do not add any extra moisture. Roll out thinly, prick with a fork and cut into fingers. Place the fingers on the baking sheet and bake for about 15-20 minutes until golden brown in colour.

METRIC CONVERSIONS

The weights, measures and oven temperatures used in the preceding recipes can be easily converted to their metric equivalents. The conversions listed below are only approximate, having been rounded up or down as may be appropriate.

Weights

Avoirdupois	Metric
1 oz.	just under 30 grams
4 oz. (¼ lb.)	app. 115 grams
8 oz. (½ lb.)	app. 230 grams
1 lb.	454 grams

Liquid Measures

Imperial	Metric
1 tablespoon (liquid only)	20 millilitres
1 fl. oz.	app. 30 millilitres
1 gill (¼ pt.)	app. 145 millilitres
½ pt.	app. 285 millilitres
1 pt.	app. 570 millilitres
1 qt.	app. 1.140 litres

Oven Temperatures

	°Fahrenheit	Gas Mark	°Celsius
Slow	300	2	150
	325	3	170
Moderate	350	4	180
	375	5	190
	400	6	200
Hot	425	7	220
	450	8	230
	475	9	240

Flour as specified in these recipes refers to Plain flour unless otherwise described.